UNIVERSITY OF MINNESOTA

⌐ *Herman Melville*

BY LEON HOWARD

UNIVERSITY OF MINNESOTA PRESS · MINNEAPOLIS

Printed in the United States of America at the North Central
Publishing Company, St. Paul

Library of Congress Catalog Card Number: 61-63842

second printing 1963

813.4
M531xho

Distributed to high schools in the United States by
McGraw-Hill Book Company, Inc.
New York   Chicago   Corte Madera, Calif.   Dallas

PUBLISHED IN GREAT BRITAIN, INDIA, AND PAKISTAN BY THE OXFORD
UNIVERSITY PRESS, LONDON, BOMBAY, AND KARACHI, AND IN
CANADA BY THOMAS ALLEN, LTD., TORONTO

HERMAN MELVILLE

LEON HOWARD is a professor of English at the University of California at Los Angeles. Among his books are *Herman Melville: A Biography* and *Literature and the American Tradition*.

⊀ Herman
Melville

Herman Melville was born in 1819, died in 1891, and has been adopted by the twentieth century as a writer peculiarly its own. Heir to the great tradition of Romantic literature, he wrote realistically of life at sea and became a popular storyteller who responded to the cultural conflicts of the mid-nineteenth century with such shrewd and passionate ambivalence that his own age eventually found him incomprehensible and left his writings for a later generation to interpret in almost as many ways as there are readers. From the outbreak of the American Civil War until the end of World War I he was an almost completely forgotten writer. Now he is one of his country's most widely read, frequently discussed, and greatly admired authors.

The familiar image of Melville today is that of all his surviving portraits — bearded, formal, and reserved, as though he were holding himself aloof from a world of getting and spending and wasted powers. It is easy to imagine him as the author of the book which puzzles and challenges his latest critic. It is less easy to imagine him as the boy who went to sea in order to escape the boredom of rural school teaching, who signed himself up for a whaling voyage on Christmas Day because he could not get a respectable job as a legal scrivener, who deserted his ship to live among cannibals, and who was to date his intellectual development from his twenty-fifth year and write *Moby Dick* at the age of thirty-one. There is a mystery about the man as well as about his works which teases and excites the imagination.

5

For a century, until recent scholarly investigations, the actual events of his life were so obscure that readers of his autobiographical romances were unable to tell whether specific statements were fact or fiction. He was born to adversity on August 1, 1819, in New York City, where his father was a well-to-do importer whose business was severely damaged by the scarcity of foreign exchange during America's first postwar depression. After eleven years of struggle Allan Melville moved his family (by then consisting of his wife, Maria Gansevoort Melville, and their eight children, of whom Herman was the third child and the second of four boys) to Albany, where Herman attended the Academy for two short years of formal education before his father's death forced him to find employment in a bank. Less than two more years of schooling, before he reached the age of eighteen, prepared him for the simple duties of elementary school teaching and the literary career he was to follow — although, like Benjamin Franklin before him, he engaged in a considerable amount of self-education by joining a young men's literary and debating society and contributing to the local newspaper in the village of Lansingburgh to which his widowed mother had moved.

In the summer of 1839 the attraction which the sea held for both the Melville and the Gansevoort members of his family induced him to make a trial voyage to Liverpool as a merchant sailor, and during the following summer he tried his inland fortune by traveling west to the lead mines around Galena, Illinois, where an uncle had settled. Another severe financial depression, however, had preceded as well as driven him westward, and he was forced to return to New York and shave his whiskers in order to look like a Christian (as his older brother put it) while vainly attempting to impose his abominable handwriting upon some lawyer in need of a clerk. Something like the desperation he was later to attribute to Ishmael, the narrator of *Moby Dick* — a damp, drizzly November

6

of the soul — caused him to join a whaling voyage to the South Pacific, for a whaler in those days was the last refuge for criminals and castaways. But Melville was free, white, and twenty-one — a sturdy, energetic young man of five feet nine and a half whose blue eyes could twinkle with humor beneath his father's high brow and waving brown hair. Desperate though he may have been in committing himself to an undefined voyage of three years or more, he was still interested in adventure when he sailed out of New Bedford on the new ship *Acushnet* on Sunday, January 3, 1841.

His voyage took him to Rio, around Cape Horn, up the coast of South America to the Galápagos Islands, and for cruises along the Line before Melville and a friend found conditions intolerable and deserted in the Marquesas on July 9, 1842. By mistake they took refuge in the valley of the Typees, who were notorious as a tribe of cannibals, and Melville remained in captivity for a month before being rescued by an Australian whaler, the *Lucy Ann*. An ailing captain, drunken mate, and mutinous crew made conditions worse on the *Lucy Ann* than they had been on the *Acushnet*; and when the vessel put into Papeete, on September 20, Melville refused further duty. He was placed under shore arrest and brought to trial but allowed to escape after his ship sailed on October 15. With one of his shipmates he then went to the neighboring island of Moorea, or Eimeo, where the two men remained as wandering beachcombers until November 3 when the master of the *Charles and Henry*, out of Nantucket, hired Melville as a harpooner for the run to the next port. After an uneventful voyage he was discharged in Lahaina, in the Hawaiian Islands, on May 2, 1843, and made his way to Honolulu where he decided to settle down as a clerk in a drygoods store for at least a year. The promise of a quick voyage home, however, persuaded him to sign on board the U.S. frigate *United States* on August 17. But it was not until early October of the following year that the ship reached Boston and

Melville was discharged and allowed to rejoin his family in Lansingburgh, where they welcomed him with relief and listened with
enthusiasm to the stories of his adventures.

Out of these stories grew his first book, *Typee: A Peep at Polynesian Life*, to give it its American title — which might have some
relationship to the spirit in which it was composed. For Melville
seems already to have been the good storyteller who was later to
astound Mrs. Nathaniel Hawthorne with his vividness, and his
sisters and their friends were good listeners who thrilled to his
dangers and could be easily teased by ambiguous references to
South Sea maidens who were as charming as any from Lansingburgh or Boston but whose impulses (as everybody knew) were
considerably less inhibited. Furthermore, the Typees were widely
known as man-eaters, and although Melville had never known a
human being to pass their lips he was not averse to taking advan-
tage of their reputation for the sake of suspense. From the very
beginning Melville played a game with his audience as he strung
out his stories to book length with picturesque descriptions, details
from memory, and other details gathered from reference books.

The game was continued, in another way and by force of cir-
cumstances, when his older brother, appointed to a diplomatic
post in London, took the manuscript with him to England and
submitted it to John Murray whose imprint could be expected to
guarantee the success of an American edition. Murray was willing
to accept it for his Home and Colonial Library (which was adver-
tised to consist of books as exciting as fiction, but all true) if he
and his readers could be assured of its authenticity. Gansevoort
Melville gave his personal assurance that his younger brother was
not "a practised writer," as Murray suspected, but a genuine sailor,
and Herman undertook to provide three new chapters and additional revisions and details which enabled the book to be published

as a sober two-volume *Narrative of a Four Months' Residence among the Natives of a Valley of the Marquesas Islands* on February 27 and April 1, 1846. In the interim, on March 17, it was published in New York under its more lively American title. It was an immediate success in both countries, and Melville was so assured of the fact in advance that he began working at once on its sequel.

He had learned something from his publishers, and *Omoo*, the sequel, was a more carefully calculated narrative. It was less teasing than *Typee*, more straightforward and convincing as a narrative of real experience, more coherent in its tone of humorous realism; and its characters, especially the narrator's companion Dr. Long Ghost, seemed drawn for a popular comic illustrator. Yet in substance it was the same sort of book *Typee* had been — a combination of memory, imagination, and research in which the author used the same device of extending each week of his real adventures into a month in order to be plausible about what might have happened to him. Because its factual background has been better established by scholars, *Omoo* in fact gives a better indication than *Typee* of the nature of young Melville's literary imagination. All he wrote was focused upon the actuality of experience, but he wrote less about what had happened to him than about what he might have experienced had he participated more fully in the events he knew about. Both books were products of that area of consciousness where memory and imagination blend and are controlled only by the desire to tell a good but convincing tale.

In the meantime, before *Omoo* was completed in December 1846 and published in the following spring, Melville was being attacked from two sides — quietly for his romance and vociferously for his realism. John Murray continued to be suspicious of *Typee* and kept insisting upon documentary proof of its veracity. So Melville was triumphant when his fellow deserter from the *Acushnet*, Rich-

9

ard Tobias Greene, appeared and offered to authenticate the narrative up to the time of his earlier escape from the Typees. "The Story of Toby" was consequently published by Murray as a separate pamphlet and then added to subsequent editions of the book. The other objection was met by suppressing certain of the realistic details in later editions. Melville had been quite candid in his criticisms of the behavior of missionaries and the social effects of their activities in the South Seas and had commented with a sailor's matter-of-factness upon the customary behavior of native females on visiting ships. The storm raised against him, in the United States, as a "traducer of missions" led to the publication of a second, expurgated, edition of his book by his American publisher, Wiley and Putnam, and his transfer to the Harpers for the publication of *Omoo* and his later novels.

His next book and first actual novel, however, was to be a problem. He had based *Typee* upon his experiences in the Marquesas and *Omoo* upon those in Tahiti, and although he had deliberately excluded any account of the whale fishery from these books he had no pattern, at the moment, for using the material which was later to go into *Moby Dick*. He was telling, with great success, a continued story of adventure while exploiting the novelty of the South Seas (which had not before been treated in fiction), and he had no more adventures of the same sort to recount. His voyage on the *Charles and Henry* had been uneventful and unprovocative. He would have to invent a series of incidents which, for the first time, would be entirely unrelated to any core of personal experience. He may have been doubtful of his ability to do so, for before he went back to his writing he rallied his friends and visited Washington in an attempt to get a job in the Treasury Department. When the attempt failed he took up his pen again with more forced energy than persuasiveness.

The impulse behind Melville's energy at this time was matrimonial. He had been courting Elizabeth Shaw, daughter of the chief justice of Massachusetts and one of his sisters' friends who had listened to him tell the tales of *Typee*, and he wanted to settle in a larger place than Lansingburgh. He had been spending an increasing amount of time in New York City, becoming acquainted with the complexities of the publishing world and finding congenial associates in the literary circle gathered around the scholarly editor Evert Duyckinck. In turn, Duyckinck found him a promising contributor of comic articles to *Yankee Doodle* and serious reviews to the new *Literary World*. Removal to the city made sense for a man who was being compelled to become a professional writer. Accordingly, after his marriage on August 4, 1847, he borrowed money to buy a house large enough for his whole family — his wife and his mother, his four unmarried sisters, his younger brother Allan and his bride, and his youngest brother Thomas who at the age of seventeen had already been two years away from home on a whaler. There, at 103 Fourth Avenue, he settled down in late September to throw himself with enthusiasm into the world of literature and begin working again on the manuscript of his third book.

The new book, eventually called *Mardi*, was to be neither a popular nor an artistic success, but its composition provides an extraordinary illustration of the growth of an artist's mind. The basic reason for its failure is structural, because it represents an unresolved conflict between Melville's conscious effort to find a unifying narrative corresponding to the picaresque sort he had been using and his unconscious compulsion to relate his writing to his own experiences which were now predominantly literary and intellectual. For the unschooled author began reading widely and avidly during this period, and his writing reflected his reading — Dante and Rabelais, Spenser and other Elizabethans, Robert Burton and Sir Thomas Browne, La Motte-Fouqué and other German

11

romancers, Coleridge and the English Romantics, and philosophers from Seneca to David Hartley. The early chapters in which he attempted to invent adventures like those in *Typee* and *Omoo* soon gave way to a more romantic but still adventurous interlude and this in turn to a sort of satiric travelogue in which a group of type characters discoursed, according to type, on the world around them as it was portrayed symbolically in the form of a South Sea archipelago called Mardi. The narrator's companion (corresponding to Toby and Long Ghost) was abandoned entirely after the romantic interlude, when the author departed completely from the pattern of his earlier books, but a certain connection was kept between the interlude and the travelogue by making the beautiful maiden introduced in the first the object of a quest in the second.

Incoherent though all this seems and is, there was a certain imaginative focal point for it within Melville's immediate experience. Books had become more exciting to him than cannibals and whales, and he was actually recording, while trying to do something else, his adventures among books. The quest reflected La Motte-Fouqué's quest in *Undine* and in *Sintram and His Companions*, Spenser's Red Crosse Knight's quest for Holinesse, and the Rabelaisian quest for the Holy Bottle. His use of allegory came from these writers, especially Spenser, and others — including the compilers of popular books on the meaning of flowers. His eccentricities of manner and style were often those of Burton's *Anatomy of Melancholy* and of Sir Thomas Browne. And one of the companions on the quest was specifically created to express his new philosophical interests. The result, inevitably, was chaos, but the apparent chaos was the turbulent effect of a vigorous mind exploring a new world which it was to conquer and control.

The tendency toward control, in fact, is evident in *Mardi* itself. For as the book progressed Melville's mind became increasingly critical and speculative. He had made his quest an allegorical search for happiness in which the hero was led forward by pure desire and driven from behind by the threat of danger from the consequences of a past action. And he had evidently decided from the beginning that happiness was not to be found in the sensuous temptations of anything like Spenser's Bower of Bliss. But at some point in his writing the quest quit being a casual narrative device holding together his random thoughts and opinions and acquired, instead, an intellectual seriousness. Religion especially interested him as a potential source of happiness, but not the institutionalized religion which he examined and rejected in the book as he had already rejected it in his actual observations on missionaries in the South Seas. Yet he allowed his philosophical companion to take refuge in the allegorical island of Serenia, where the dictates of reason and of Christian charity were one; and eventually his historian and poet were also directed there, while his representative ruler renounced all thought of happiness and returned to his turbulent country. But the hero and narrator, Taji, was more Romantic: his was an endless quest as he pursued his intangible goal, followed by the specters of his past, "over an endless sea."

This was the book as Melville thought he had completed it on the eve of the French Revolution in the spring of 1848. But the intellectual development revealed in it was not yet complete. For when news of the events in Europe reached him Melville's imagination was stirred, as it had never been before, by the signs of immediate social change, and he increased the size of his book one-sixth by the insertion of some twenty-three chapters of political allegory. These referred to the revolutions in France (Franko) and other parts of Europe (Porpheero), to the Chartist movement and the international and fiscal policies of England (Dominora), to the problems created by slavery and by geographical expansion in the United States (Vivenza), and to various other matters ranging from the potato famine in Ireland to conditions in India. They reveal an extraordinary perceptiveness, in depth, to the long-range significance of contemporary events; and perhaps the most interesting of these chapters, from this point of view, are those in which he anticipated the social consequences attendant on the closing of the American frontier and on the California gold rush which had not yet occurred at the time he wrote. The young man who had so recently moved to the city and entered the larger world of the mind had acquired an unusual amount of knowledge, understanding, and vision in a remarkably short time.

Melville had also acquired something else while writing *Mardi* which he did not recognize or appreciate. He knew before the book was published in March 1849 (by Bentley, in London, for Murray had refused it) that it would be a failure, and financial necessity compelled him to return at once to his old successful vein — the autobiographical romance. The richest of its novelties, his South Sea adventures, had been exhausted, except for the whaling materials, but he still had the events of his trip to Liverpool which he worked into *Redburn: His First Voyage* and completed by the end of June. He always spoke of it as a book he despised and may actually have done so. He knew that so many men had written of their youthful experiences before the mast that the subject was hackneyed, and he knew, too, that he could not afford to put into this book the sort of intellectual and literary excitement which had damned *Mardi* as a commercial venture. But he did not know that the emotions he felt while writing could be projected into the past or into a fiction in a way that would give his words a vitality which he himself did not associate with the intentional context of meaning.

With *Redburn* Melville became a novelist — so persuasively so, in fact, that many later readers have had difficulty accepting the evidence that he himself was some four years older than his hero when he first went to sea and that the most memorable parts of the book are pure fiction. It is true that most of the characters in the novel were Melville's actual companions, some under their real names, on his first voyage. But Jackson, the most memorable of them because of his strange hold over the crew and his dramatic death, was alive at the end of a trip which included no casualties of any sort. Melville himself was by no means the timid, under-sized innocent who serves as the narrator, nor did the ship carry immigrants or the plague on its return voyage. Yet the personality of the narrator and the circumstantial accounts of the outbreak of a virulent disease in a crowded steerage seem to reflect an emotional involvement which makes the book more convincing than either *Typee* or *Omoo*.

The probability is that Melville was more deeply involved in *Redburn* than in his earlier books but that it was the involvement of the moment, not of the past through memory. Wellingborough Redburn may have been not at all like Herman Melville but he could very easily be an older brother's affectionate representation of Thomas Melville who had gone to sea at the age of fifteen, who had recently returned and left again on a voyage to China, and who was so much on Herman's mind that *Redburn* was dedicated to him. And if Melville's own return from Liverpool had not been on a plague ship crowded with immigrants, he was nevertheless writing the latter part of his book while the blue cholera was creating panic in New York after having been brought there by an immigrant ship the preceding December. The unregulated conditions on board such ships were notorious, and Melville knew the slums from which their passengers came. A man whose imagination and emotions could be deeply stirred by contemporary events (as Melville's had been when he wrote the political chapters of *Mardi*) may readily have undertaken, out of a sort of indignant humanitarianism, to make the public realize that it was suffering from its own indifference to the welfare of the less fortunate. "For the whole world is the patrimony of the whole world," he wrote with reference to the agitated question of whether "multitudes of foreign poor should be landed on our American shores"; "there is no telling who does not own a stone in the Great Wall of China." *Redburn* is a convincing book because the emotions which controlled it were genuine, profound, and pervasive enough to affect its style: the writing in the first part reflects the simplicity of his involvement in a boy's point of view, whereas that of the last half has the detachment of an observer who realizes the significance of what he is writing about.

But Melville had no time, at the moment, to realize the significance of his literary achievement. He was heavily in debt and turned at once to a book based on his naval experience, writing *White Jacket* at the rate of nearly three thousand words a day during July and August while reading proofs on *Redburn* and a new edition of *Typee*. Once again he used real people, drawn out of his memory, as characters, but most of the events of the voyage around Cape Horn were fictitious. He borrowed freely from various sources the numerous comic incidents which were sprinkled through it, but what he called its "man-of-warish" style was a holdover from the indignant humanitarianism of *Redburn*. Some of his indignation was undoubtedly a reflection of his past resentment against the arbitrary restraints and cruelties of naval life, and his brutal ship's surgeon, though perhaps real enough, belonged to a literary tradition that went back to Smollett. But the abolition of flogging was being agitated at the time he wrote, and the pervasive theme of his emphasis upon it as an unnecessarily cruel but all-too-usual punishment was in the interest of reform. Both in *White Jacket* and in *Redburn* he exhibited the naturalistic impulse to portray vividly the evils of society in the hope that legislative action would be taken against them.

Yet *White Jacket* was a deeper book than its predecessor had been. Its subtitle labeled it "The World in a Man-of-War" and its concluding chapter drew an elaborate analogy between the frigate and the earth, sailing through space with clean decks and dark storerooms of secrets beneath the "lie" of its surface. For Melville had found the microcosm of his man-of-war, despite its friendly companionship of the foretop and its occasional comedy, a cruel world of arbitrary power and discipline, motiveless malice, ruthlessness, and brutality. Above all, it was a world of constraint, in which men had to swing their hammocks without "spreaders," turn on signal when they were allowed to sleep on the crowded deck, and go sleepless because precedent and convention required the storing of gear in the daytime. It was a world of absolute command from above and of mystery and subterranean darkness below. Perhaps Melville felt the constraint to an unusual degree while writing, for he had sacrificed his customary summer vacation to the book and was working through the August heat in a city so panic-stricken from the cholera that people were afraid to go outdoors or eat their customary food. Physically as well as financially, the world was pressing in upon him, and he must have felt it. At any rate, there was an incipient violence in the emotion underlying *White Jacket* which suggested that at any moment its author might break loose.

Whatever the constraint Melville may have felt during the summer was relieved in October 1849, when he decided to go abroad in an effort to get better terms for *White Jacket* than he had been able to get, by correspondence with his English publisher, for *Redburn*. He also planned to collect material for a historical novel based upon the real life of an American Revolutionary patriot who had been captured by the British and had lived for forty years in England as an exile. But the trip was to have unexpected consequences. For one thing, it renewed his sea memories. The captain of his ship gave him a private stateroom with a porthole through which he could gaze at the ocean, and he was also allowed the freedom of the rigging so that he could recapture all the old emotions of being at the masthead. For another, it proved to be an exciting intellectual experience. Two of his fellow passengers, George J. Adler and Frank Taylor, were young men of philosophical inclinations with whom he could discuss the subject which had so interested him in the concluding chapter of *White Jacket* — "Fixed Fate, Free-will, Fore-knowledge absolute." Their interest in German Transcendentalism appealed to the man who had become acquainted with Emerson, for the first time, only eight months before and had been surprised to find in him deep thoughts rather than "myths and oracular gibberish." He was to talk with them, on every occasion he could make, even after the voyage was over and he was in London and Paris.

By the time Melville returned home, on February 1, 1850, he seems to have laid aside his plan for the historical novel. At any rate, by May 1 he had seen *White Jacket* through the press and was able to write Richard Henry Dana, Jr., that he was "half way" in a book which he referred to as "the 'whaling voyage.'"And on June 27 he promised the completed volume to his English publisher "in the later part of the coming autumn" and described it specifically but with some exaggeration as "a romance of adventure, founded upon certain wild legends in the Southern Sperm Whale Fisheries and illustrated by the author's own personal experience, of two years and more, as a harpooneer." In the middle of July he was ready for a vacation and left for Pittsfield, Massachusetts, where Evert Duyckinck visited him in early August and wrote that "Melville has a new book mostly done — a romantic, fanciful and literal and most enjoyable presentment of the Whale Fishery — something quite new."

These early references to the book which was to become *Moby*

Dick are of unusual interest because they introduce the most teasing question which arises in any effort to follow the development of Melville's creative imagination: How did it happen that he was to spend a year of agonized composition upon a "mostly done" manuscript and transform it from a romance with autobiographical overtones into the powerfully dramatic novel it became? He seems to have had no intention, when he went on his vacation, of doing more than filling out his narrative with realistic details gathered from books of reference he had collected for that purpose. But once again the emotions of immediate experience were to project themselves into his fiction, transform it, and give it — this time — not only the vitality of his own life but the tensions of the century in which he lived.

The trigger action for his explosion into greatness was that of a single day, August 5, 1850, during his vacation when one of his neighbors arranged an expedition and dinner party for all the literary celebrities of the region — the New Englanders who summered in the Berkshires and Melville and the New York guests he had invited up for a visit. The expedition was to the top of Monument Mountain where Melville, Nathaniel Hawthorne, and Oliver Wendell Holmes were made gay by the elevation and champagne and brought back to sobriety by the New York critic Cornelius Mathews, who insisted upon making the occasion literary by reading William Cullen Bryant's solemn poem about the Indian lovers who had leaped to their death from the projecting ledge on which Melville had been performing sailor's antics. Holmes's satiric impulses were aroused, and the result was a literary quarrel which continued throughout the "well moistened" dinner party later. It focused upon the theory of the influence of climate upon genius and the question whether America would produce a literature as elevated as its mountains and as spacious as its plains. The New Englanders (as Holmes's Phi Beta Kappa poem *Astraea* of a few days later was to show) were skeptical of the New Yorkers' enthusiasm.

Melville's part in the argument seems to have been more mischievous than serious, but he was impressed by it and even more impressed by his first meeting with Hawthorne. His aunt had given him a copy of *Mosses from an Old Manse* at the beginning of his vacation, but he had not yet read it. Now, having met the author, he read it with the extraordinary enthusiasm he expressed in the belated review he wrote for the *Literary World* before his New York friends went home. Hawthorne proved the greatness of American literature, he contended, under the anonymous signature of "A Virginian spending July in Vermont"; but it was a greatness of heart and mind, observable in Hawthorne's willingness to present the "blackness" of truth — the same dark "background against which Shakespeare plays his grandest conceits" and which "appeals to that Calvinistic sense of Innate Depravity and Original Sin, from whose visitations, in some shape or other, no deeply thinking mind is always and wholly free." In Hawthorne and his *Mosses* Melville found an attitude of mind which courageously reflected all his doubts concerning the Transcendental idealism and optimism that had interested him during his recent voyage and had affected his reading since.

The impression made by Hawthorne was so great that Melville cultivated his acquaintance assiduously during the following months and eventually dedicated *Moby Dick* to him. Yet he did not become a wholehearted convert to his new friend's "black" skepticism. He was himself a man of greater vitality, more of a man of action, than Hawthorne; and although the two shared an interest in the Gothic Romance, Hawthorne's interest was in the Gothic atmosphere whereas Melville's was in the Romantic hero — the Byronic wandering outlaw of his own dark mind. Furthermore, Melville had borrowed *Sartor Resartus* at the time he finished collecting his whaling library for the revision of his book, and he found in Carlyle's Transcendentalized version of the Romantic hero a character who was as "deep-diving" as Emerson but who had proved himself susceptible to Hawthorne's pessimism and capable of defying it. In one of his stories in the *Mosses*, "Earth's Holocaust," Hawthorne had set forth allegorically his belief that evil could not be destroyed because it was constantly being re-created by "the all-engendering heart of man." Melville was inclined to agree. But the best "strong positive illustration" Melville found of the "blackness in Hawthorne" was in the story of "Young Goodman Brown" and his allegorical but unanswered cry for "Faith." In Carlyle's book Melville found a hero who could live in such a spiritual state of "starless, Tartarean black" that he could hear the Devil say "thou art fatherless, outcast, and the Universe is mine" but who still had the courage and the energy to say *"I am not thine, but Free, and forever hate thee!"* Whether he was as sensible as Young Goodman Brown (who went into a lethargy when he was convinced, either by a dream or by a real experience, that the world was the Devil's) might be questionable. But he was more heroic and, to Melville's mind, more admirable.

Melville's literary interests, in short, reveal the tensions that existed in his mind at the time he began what otherwise might have been the routine job of revising his manuscript. They were vital tensions, not only in terms of his own sensitivity but in their profound effect upon Western civilization during the nineteenth century — tensions set up by the conflict between the will to believe and the need to be shown, between Transcendentalism and empiricism in philosophy, between religion and science, between faith and skepticism. These were not tensions to be resolved, as so many of Melville's contemporaries tried to resolve them, for no satisfactory resolution has yet proved possible. Melville, at his deepest and most complex creative level, made no attempt to resolve the conflict. Instead, he dramatized it. And it may be that the ambiguity and ambivalence inherent in the dramatic Shakespearean qualities of *Moby Dick* are responsible for the fact that it has a greater appeal to the puzzled and questioning twentieth century than do the writings of Melville's contemporaries who were more explicitly concerned with the same tensions.

In any event, Shakespeare was an important element in the literary and intellectual ferment which went into the making of *Moby Dick*. Melville had become excited about him at the time he discovered Transcendentalism, in February 1849, when he wrote Evert Duyckinck that "if another Messiah ever comes twill be in Shakspeare's person." And he kept looking, in his review of the *Mosses*, if not for another Messiah at least for another Shakespeare — perhaps "this day being born on the banks of the Ohio." Hawthorne had "approached" him, for a nineteenth-century Shakespeare would not be an Elizabethan dramatist but a part of his "times" with "correspondent coloring." There is no doubt but that Melville was excited by the company and the literary debate of August 5, 1850, and it may have been that this excitement was intensified by a feeling of challenge. Within a few days he was to denounce the "absolute and unconditional adoration of Shakspeare" and his "unapproachability" as one of "our Anglo-Saxon superstitions." Might not he himself be another man "to carry republican progressiveness into Literature as well as into Life" by writing a novel that had the quality of Shakespearean tragedy?

However this might be, his novel began to change from a story of the whale fishery to a story of "the Whale." Captain Ahab (named for a man who had "done evil in the sight of the Lord") remained the protagonist in his narrative, but his antagonist was neither the worthy mate Starbuck nor any member of his exotic crew. It was the great white whale with a humped back and hieroglyphics on his brow, known throughout the fishery as Moby Dick and notorious for the viciousness with which he had turned upon the men who had hunted and attempted to destroy him. Ahab himself had been his victim on a previous voyage when the whale had sheared off his leg and started a train of cause and effect that resulted in his further mutilation by its splintered substitute. And Ahab, a queer "grand, ungodly, god-like man," had embarked on a voyage of revenge which would follow the paths of the migrating leviathan throughout the vast Pacific until he and the whole ship's crew were destroyed and the narrator alone was left to tell the tale. In order to make the voyage plausible Melville had to draw upon the whole body of available whaling lore in extraordinary detail. He also had to made his captain mad.

But the power of the book does not come from the realistic fantasy of the voyage or from the obsessed madness of the traditional Gothic or Romantic protagonist who is half hero and half villain. On the contrary, it comes from the fact that Ahab is one of the few characters in literature genuinely "formed for noble tragedies." Like Lear, he is a noble individual whose only flaw is a single mistake in judgment. And like Hamlet, at least as Coleridge interpreted him, his mistake is that of a disordered judgment — that of a man with a "craving after the indefinite" who "looks upon external things as hieroglyphics" and whose mind, with its "everlasting broodings," is "unseated from its healthy relation" and "constantly occupied with the world within, and abstracted from the world without — giving substance to shadows, and throwing a mist over all commonplace actualities." For to Ahab "all visible objects" were "but as pasteboard masks" from behind which "some unknown but still reasoning thing puts forth the mouldings of its features." To him the white whale was the emblem of "outrageous strength, with inscrutable malice sinewing it"; and it was "that inscrutable thing" which he hated, and he was determined to "wreak that hate upon him."

23

Whether Ahab's attitude should be interpreted in psychological or philosophical terms is an important question with respect to Melville's biography. The narrator, Ishmael, uses psychological terms in his accounts of the phases Ahab goes through while "deliriously transferring" his idea of evil to the whale as an object which would visibly personify it and make it practically assailable. Ahab himself, of course, sounds like Carlyle's hero asserting his individual freedom and defying the Devil's claim to the universe. The weight of the evidence, derived from the book and from letters written at the same time, appears to favor a rather close identification of the author's point of view with that of the narrator. Melville's conscious fable in *Moby Dick* seems to lead to the conclusion that a belief in the emblematic nature of the universe is a form of madness. His rational judgment apparently concurred with that of Hawthorne: the white whale was a natural beast, and the evil in him was a product of the "all-engendering heart" or mind of Ahab. But, for the moment, Melville's personal philosophy is not relevant to an interpretation of *Moby Dick* as a work of literature. "Dramatically regarded," as he himself put it, "all men tragically great are made so through a certain morbidness." The important point is that Ahab's "morbidness," whether a sane conviction or a mad obsession, was the tragic flaw in his character which directed his heroic behavior toward destruction.

Yet if one goes beyond superficial interpretation into an attempt to explain the strange power of *Moby Dick*, Melville's personal beliefs do become important and his chapter on "The Whiteness of the Whale" becomes particularly relevant. For here he collects evidence for the existence of a sort of knowledge which is more intuitive than the rational empiricism used by Ishmael to explain "crazy Ahab" in the immediately preceding chapter. The inference to be drawn is that Melville was not wholly convinced of the validity of the fable his rational mind constructed in order to provide himself with a plot of the sort he found and admired in Hawthorne. The conflict between Transcendentalism and empiricism was not something which he merely observed and then dramatized. It was something that he experienced and felt deeply within himself. Ahab, who sometimes doubted whether there was anything beyond the "wall" of the emblematic material universe, was only slightly more mad than the storyteller who condemned him but sometimes doubted whether the material world of experience provided the ultimate form of knowledge. Melville could easily imagine within himself the rage to believe, the madness, he attributed to his hero as a "tragic flaw."

In fact, if one explores the creative level which lies beneath an artist's identification with the intellectual and emotional conflicts of his age, there is abundant evidence of a deeply rooted desire in Melville to be as heroically mad as Ahab. Such evidence is to be found in his imagery. The image of the fatherless outcast had been a controlling one in his earlier books. He had been the deserter in *Typee*, the runaway in *Omoo*, the escaped captive in *Mardi*, the orphan in *Redburn*, and the poor sailor denied a charitable daub of paint in *White Jacket*. And in *Moby Dick* he was Ishmael, the homeless wanderer. The image, of course, was that of his own life from the time he left school at his father's death until he married, bought a house, and established himself in New York. But in *White Jacket*, as we have seen, a new and conflicting image began to emerge and become dominant — that of constraint and subterranean mystery, with emotional overtones of incipient violence. The loss of his wandering bachelor's freedom, his crowded household, his serious financial problems, and the peculiar cooped-up desperation of his writing *Redburn* and *White Jacket* during the plague may have all contributed to its emergence. But its origin probably was in something deeper — in the feeling of growth, so vividly expressed in a letter to Hawthorne in June 1851, which made him believe that what he was most moved to write was banned and that all his books were "botches." He felt himself one of those "deep men" who had something "eating in them" and frustrating them. It was time for him to deny his fatherless, outcast state and assert his freedom, like Carlyle's hero, with his "whole Me." Looking at all the things that hemmed him in, he might well suspect that "there's naught beyond" but still cry with Ahab "How can the prisoner reach outside except by thrusting through the wall?"

The imagery of constraint, frustration, and the obscure mystery of frustration is so pervasive in *Moby Dick* that one is almost compelled to believe that the secret of its vitality lies somewhere in Melville's own heroic attempt, by using all the resources of language and invention he could command, to thrust through the wall of frustrations he could not fully understand. "I have a sort of sea-feeling," he had written Evert Duyckinck in December 1850, when the ground was covered with snow. "My room seems a ship's cabin; and at nights when I wake up and hear the wind shrieking, I almost fancy there is too much sail on the house, and I had better go on the roof and rig in the chimney." And at the end of the following June, when the book was half through the press, he wrote Hawthorne of his disgust "with the heat and dust of the babylonish brick-kiln of New York" and his return to the country "to feel the grass — and end the book reclining on it." It was only natural, perhaps, that he should have also written Hawthorne that the book was baptized (like Ahab's harpoon) in the name of the Devil, for there was a great deal of Ahab's passion in Melville while he wrote.

Moby Dick was completed shortly before its author's thirty-second birthday and published in London on October 18, 1851, and in New York about four weeks later. Hawthorne understood the fable, and his understanding gave Melville, for a moment, "a sense of unspeakable security" and an awareness of more pervasive allegorical implications than he had intended. But the book was not a success. Although the reviews were better, the sales were no greater than those of *Mardi*. Once again Melville had to face the fact that if he poured his whole self into a book it was almost certainly doomed to commercial failure.

While he was writing *Moby Dick* Melville's way of life was drastically changed. He had bought a house, Arrowhead, and a hundred and fifty acres of ground in the Berkshires, and he had set himself up as a farmer. There his second son was born during the autumn of 1851, and there, during the winter, he contemplated his next literary project. Hawthorne's appreciation of *Moby Dick* in November had stirred his ambition: "Leviathan is not the biggest fish," he had written; " — I have heard of Krakens." But by January 1852 he apparently faced the fact that he would make very little money from the sort of books he wanted to write and decided that, if dollars damned him, he would go ahead and be damned. He would try to do something that would be popular. And so he wrote Mrs. Hawthorne (who had surprised him by liking the whaling story) that he would not again send her "a bowl of salt water" but "a rural bowl of milk." He offered the new book to his English publisher, Richard Bentley, soon afterward; and when Bentley cited his losses on the earlier books as an argument in favor of a contract for half-profits instead of a substantial advance, Melville suggested that he "let bygones be bygones" and publish the new work under an assumed name such as "Guy Winthrop." For it was "very much more calculated for popularity than anything you have yet published of mine — being a regular romance, with a mysterious plot to it, and stirring passions at work, and withall, representing a new and elevated aspect of American life."

By this time, April 16, 1852, the rapidly written book was completed and in type at his American publisher's, and it is difficult to understand how its author could have written about it in such terms. For this "rural bowl of milk" was *Pierre; or, The Ambiguities*, surely the most perverse of Melville's novels in its unrestrained imagination, about which Bentley worried, and its offensiveness to the "many sensitive readers" with whom he was concerned. It was probably planned as a sort of satiric variation on the *Moby Dick* fable in a situation and setting which would have a greater appeal to feminine readers. Its hero, Pierre Glendinning, was a sophomoric version of Captain Ahab who also had his vision of the absolute and acted accordingly. But Pierre's intuition was of good rather than evil — of an absolute morality superior to that of the everyday world which surrounded even his idyllic existence with an affectionate widowed mother on a large country estate. It led him, when he became convinced that a strange dark girl in the vicinity was his illegitimate half-sister, to pretend marriage with her in order that she might have the Glendinning name without disturbing his mother's devotion to his father's memory. And it also led him to disinheritance, to a fantastic existence in New York City as a writer among a group of Transcendental Apostles, and to a tragic end which was more melodramatic than that of Captain Ahab.

Melville may have persuaded himself while trying (in vain) to sell the book to Bentley that he had managed to combine genial satire with the mysterious plot and passions of the Gothic romances which had so interested him during the early stages of writing *Moby Dick*. But if he did he was ignoring the fact that the major — and, from a commercial point of view, the most damning — ambiguity in *Pierre* reflected his compulsive desire to resolve the emotional and intellectual conflict which had made *Moby Dick* so effectively dramatic. Did Pierre Glendinning deserve any sympathy at all for his immature behavior while pursuing some ideal of absolute morality? Was there any validity in the sort of evidence for intuitive knowledge that Melville had assembled the year before for his chapter on "The Whiteness of the Whale"? Or was a person who believed in the Transcendental absolute simply fooling himself? By presenting Ahab as an obsessed madman, he had made the answer to such questions as these a matter of opinion rather than one for investigation; and he had expressed his own rational opinion in the fable of the book. But the questions continued to haunt him.

For Pierre was not mad. He was very young and very foolish but in no sense neurotic, obsessed, or crazy. And Melville could not resist the impulse to explore the psychology of his behavior, following "the endless, winding way" (as he put it) of "the flowing river in the cave of man" wherever it might lead in a manner that would not be permitted in a "mere novel." He did it with an honesty and a subtlety which resulted in the first genuine psychological novel in American literature. But the way led him to the ruinous theme of incest. At the beginning he had made the dark Isabel beautiful in order to keep Pierre from seeming too perfect and immaculate: his hero would have been less ready to "champion the right," Melville observed, had he not been invited to do so by beauty rather than ugliness. His intention had been to make her beauty one of those "mere contingent things" of which Pierre would be unaware while it served the artistic purpose of keeping the "heavenly fire" of his enthusiasm within a plausible vessel of human "clay." But Melville's years at sea and in strange lands had given him a greater understanding of human frailty than of Victorian proprieties, and he allowed the "contingent" attraction of Isabel to develop beyond the limits of discretion before the book reached its melodramatic conclusion. Once more he had gone too far in putting too much serious thought into a book designed for popular consumption.

He had also gone beyond simple indiscretion. For *Pierre* shows signs of strains and tensions quite different from those in *Moby Dick*. It contains less ambivalence and more indications of conflicting purpose. The superficial romanticism of its idyllic episodes and mysterious plot was calculated to make it a popular novel, but the serious probing into psychological depths represented the kind of speculation that had been widely condemned in *Mardi* and *Moby Dick*. The amused detachment with which Pierre was treated as a "sophomore" probably represented an effort to achieve the "genialities" Melville admired in Hawthorne, but the amusement sometimes became sardonic. He drew upon his own early background to a considerable extent for the details of Pierre's, but as he approached the present a touch of bitterness crept in. His picture of Pierre at his writing plank was a comic portrayal, in Carlylese, of a desperate attempt to write the great American novel; but it was based so much upon the grim conditions under which he himself had been writing during the past three years that the comedy had to be forced and exaggerated in order to avoid the risk of self-pity. The serious elements in the book are many and varied, but they all serve to create the total effect of an author who was attempting the light touch with an uncontrollably heavy hand.

More than ever, perhaps, Melville was feeling the spiritual claustrophobia which had become evident in the summer of 1849. The image of the vault is frequent in *Pierre*, and the statue of Laocoön appears, near the middle of the book, in a niche off the stairs leading to Mrs. Glendinning's chamber. One of the most memorable incidents in the story is the section in which Pierre, in a dream, identifies himself with Enceladus, imprisoned in the earth with only the stumps of his once audacious arms, striving in vain to assault the heavens. Melville's comment on this section indicates clearly that Pierre could and did use his knowledge of old fables to elucidate his own dreams and that he found this one "most repulsively fateful and foreboding" only because he failed to wrest from it its ultimate meaning: "Whoso storms the sky gives best proof he came from thither! But whatso crawls contented in the moat before that crystal fort, shows it was born within that slime, and there forever will abide." Pierre never learned to strike the "stubborn rock" of fable "and force even aridity itself to quench his painful thirst" for self-knowledge. But Melville did, and what he learned, while writing *Pierre,* helps explain the mystery of some of his writings which were to come later.

Commercially as well as artistically *Pierre* was Melville's greatest failure. The reviewers were unanimous in condemning it, and fewer than three hundred copies were to be sold during the entire year following its publication. The wise old judge who was his father-in-law became worried as soon as he read the book. He knew that Melville was a popular writer only when he wrote about ships and sailors, and so he persuaded the young man to go with him on a trip to Nantucket where he was holding court in early July 1852. He planned to have Herman meet some of the people connected with whaling in New Bedford and Nantucket and then have a refreshing vacation at Martha's Vineyard and the Elizabeth Islands. Melville was willing to go and also to keep his eyes open for fresh literary material.

But what he found was not what Judge Shaw probably hoped for. No suggestion of adventure — either of escape or of bold defiance — came his way and fired his imagination. Instead of being impressed by the daring seafaring men of Nantucket he was impressed by the patient women of the island who waited, so often in vain, for their husbands' return from distant lands and seas. The story he brought back with him, well documented, was that of a certain Agatha Robertson whose husband had deserted her for seventeen years and then returned and deserted her again with no reproach from Agatha. The whole story and the incidents connected with it, he felt, were "instinct with significance"; but he hesitated about writing it and tried in vain to get Hawthorne to do so before he decided, with the beginning of his winter writing season in December 1852, to undertake it himself. There is no evidence that Melville ever wrote or even made a fair beginning of the Agatha story, but his interest in it and his unproductive winter are both significant in view of his preoccupation with the theme of patience when he did begin to write again.

During this period of nonproductivity his family decided that writing was bad for him and that he should apply to the new Democratic president, Hawthorne's friend and classmate, Franklin Pierce, for a diplomatic post abroad. They enlisted the help of so many friends and made such a case for the desirability of a change in occupation for him that they created a lasting impression of a nervous breakdown from "too much excitement of the imagination." But they failed to get him an appointment and failed to divert him from the profession of writing. On the contrary, Melville decided, during that winter, to turn more professional than he had ever been before. He agreed to become a contributor to the new *Putnam's Monthly Magazine* at five dollars a page (the highest price paid any of its contributors), and *Putnam's* introduced him to its readers in the issue of February 1853 as the first of "Our Young Authors." His first contribution, which, however, did not appear until November and December, was "Bartleby, the Scrivener; A Story of Wall-Street," not only the first of his short stories but one of the most interesting and revealing of all the documents in the history of Melville's imaginative life.

In the first place, "Bartleby" is a classic but unusual fable of patience — unusual because it tells of a patience which has within itself the tensions of both acceptance and defiance. Its hero is not active, like Captain Ahab or even Pierre. He is completely passive. But he is as defiant as either. He makes no attempt to storm the sky, but he does not crawl in the slime. He would simply "prefer not to" crawl or to conform to any of the expectations of him. His force of character is great but entirely negative. Furthermore, there seems to be little question but that this was a fable deliberately created by Melville in a search for self-knowledge. For the patience of Bartleby was much closer to that of his own temperament than was anything he could find in the story of Agatha or the women of Nantucket. Various real incidents may have contributed to the substance of the fable, but the powerful center of its invention seems to have been a soul-searching speculation about "what might have been." Suppose Melville had obtained and accepted a job as a lawyer's clerk instead of defiantly going to sea and writing such defiant books as *Mardi, Moby Dick,* and *Pierre.* What might his fate have been? Melville looked in his heart and wrote that it would be pretty much the same as Pierre's — death in the Tombs.

"Bartleby" is a story extraordinarily rich in its suggestiveness, but, next to its soul-searching quality, its most interesting characteristic is its conscious use of a dominant image — as though Melville, like Pierre, had been directed by his most haunting dreams to a fable that was capable of revealing his condition. The wall that Ahab saw in Moby Dick is everywhere in this "Story of Wall-Street." Bartleby faces it in his employer's office and in the exercise yard of the Tombs, and he dies quietly at its base. Pierre's dream of Enceladus was of a no more profound symbol of confinement. It was a symbol that had crept gradually into Melville's writings, probably without his awareness, but this time he used it as consciously as he might have done had he been attempting to exorcise it. He did not succeed. But as he continued to write short stories he continued to be conscious of his own feeling of frustration, to seek its possible cause, and to use his search as a device for giving meaning to the fables he created.

One such story was the otherwise trivial "Cock-a-Doodle-Doo!"

published in *Harper's Monthly Magazine* for December, in which he explained the behavior of a character similar to Bartleby in terms of pride. But he had more ambitious plans for the winter and did not continue this kind of analysis. Despite the failure of *Pierre* the Harpers were eager for another novel from him, and on December 7, 1853, they gave him an advance of $300 for a work on "Tortoises or Tortoise-Hunting" which he hoped to complete in January. He knew the Galápagos Islands well enough, from experience and through reading, to provide the background; but unfortunately he had no story, and the best he could find was that of a Chola woman who was left alone on desolate Norfolk Isle when her husband and brother died in a fishing accident. Her experience should have appealed to whatever had haunted him in the Agatha story, but he could make nothing of it. "She but showed us her soul's lid, and the strange ciphers thereon engraved," he said; "all within, with pride's timidity, was withheld." He seems to have turned to Spenser and other poets for suggestions and inspiration for an allegorical narrative of patience, but when the Harpers' publishing house burned, shortly after he received his advance, and he thought their book publishing activities would be suspended, he lost his incentive for proceeding with a difficult job. He turned his material into a series of ten sketches and sold them to *Putnam's* for serial publication, as "The Encantadas," in the spring. The whole affair was unfortunate because the Harpers were offended and Melville lost the encouragement and support of his publishers when his creative energies were at their lowest ebb.

The little additional writing Melville managed before the spring planting season touched upon the theme of frustration in economic terms. It consisted of two pairs of contrasting sketches, "The Two Temples" and "Poor Man's Pudding and Rich Man's Crumbs," and the first was particularly effective in the use it made of the imprisonment image when the poor man who was excluded from the congregation of a wealthy church became locked in the bell tower. It was rejected by *Putnam's*, however, on the grounds that it might give offense; and if Melville had any deep or serious impulse to find further social and economic symbols for the "wall" around him he repressed it. Instead, he turned in the late spring to the historical novel he had planned in 1849. *Israel Potter; or, Fifty Years of Exile* was published serially in *Putnam's* and in book form (by Putnam rather than the Harpers) in the spring of 1855. Actually, he had little personal reason to get wrought up over the world's economic distinctions. He was making a living from his farm, his bank balance was increasing, and, although he satirized the mercenary spirit of Benjamin Franklin in *Israel Potter* and the cruel salesmanship of "The Lightning Rod Man," he presented the readers of *Harper's* for July 1854 with "The Happy Failure" — a man who had worked on an invention for as long as Melville himself had worked at writing and found kindness in his heart only when his device failed.

Yet Melville did not seriously consider himself a failure, as a writer or in any other way, and during the following winter he undertook one of the most ambitious and impressive of all his literary projects. It was to be the story of a South American slave ship, bound from Valparaiso to Callao, on which the slaves revolted, killed the owner, and forced the captain to promise to take them to Africa. Based upon a real story told by a New England ship's captain, Amasa Delano, it was focused on Captain Delano's gradual realization of the situation when the South American vessel appealed to him for help. It was one Melville could handle by developing its "significances" as he had developed those in *Moby Dick*, and it quite evidently appealed strongly to his imagination. Here was all he needed to enable him to project his deepest feelings out of himself and into the characters of a fiction — the Spanish captain, Don Benito Cereno, surrounded by an ominous crowd of blacks whose leader played the role of a devoted servant but was always prepared to cut his master's throat; and the New England captain who was aware that there was something beyond the wall of his perception and to whom the mystery could be unveiled in a dramatic climax. Here were the ships and the sea that Melville knew so well, the material for the plausibly grotesque symbolism he loved, and a number of technical legal documents he could expound upon. It did not have the dramatic possibilities of *Moby Dick*, but it had the potentialities of a great novel in the Gothic tradition, historically true in fact and so close to Melville's own experience in setting that he could let his imagination control it without the risk of implausible fantasy.

He proposed the book to *Putnam's* in March 1855, but the magazine had just acquired a new publisher whose new reader advised him to "decline any novel from Melville which is not extremely good." And the advice was apparently taken, at the worst of all possible times. For Melville was still estranged from the Harpers, and he had just experienced what his wife called "his first attack of severe rheumatism in his back — so that he was helpless." He also must have been deeply discouraged because in April he sent to the magazine the portion of the book he had written, complete with legal documents but without explanation. The reader complained of the "great pity that he did not work it up as a connected tale instead of putting the dreary documents at the end" but advised its acceptance on the grounds that it was Melville's "best style of subject" although he continued to fret that he "does everything too hurriedly now." After many delays it was published as a long short story, "Benito Cereno," and only a careful comparison of Melville's version of the "dreary documents at the end" with their originals gives a clue to the full substance of the novel Melville might have written had either he or his publishers possessed greater confidence in his energy and talents.

But he continued to write, and his writings show that he continued to search his own consciousness for fables of frustration.
Marriage was one explanation he seems to have considered in "The
Paradise of Bachelors and the Tartarus of Maids" in *Harper's* for
April — although the allegory of gestation he introduced into the
second part suggests that Elizabeth's pregnancy (with their second
daughter, and fourth and last child) was more in his mind than
marriage itself. "The Bell Tower" in the August *Putnam's*, however, was more serious, because it seems to have been closely connected in his mind with "Benito Cereno" and because it seems to
be an introspective consideration of his own literary career. More
flamboyant in style than any of his other stories, it was a parable
of an overambitious architect who was destroyed by a flaw in his
own work; and, for once, Melville made his meaning plain: "So
the creator was killed by the creature. So the bell was too heavy
for the tower. So the bell's main weakness was where man's blood
had flawed it. And so pride went before the fall."

From the point of view of popular success, his own work had
been weakest when he put his human "blood" in it, and his pride
was going rapidly before the crippling illness from which he suf-
fered all summer. "I and My Chimney" (which was accepted by
Putnam's in September but not published until the following
March) is almost certainly a humorous account of the physical
examination of his injured back rather than of his mental condition as some traditions have maintained. And it is this preoccupation with physical frustration which helps explain the peculiarities
of *The Confidence Man* — the last piece of prose fiction he was to
publish during his lifetime — which he wrote during the winter
of 1855–56. The book is a double-bitted satire, attacking gullibility
in its first part and cynicism in its last, and its imagery reflects and
perhaps explains its attitude and tone. The parts first composed
(including the interpolated story of China Aster) are bitter, and

37

they are also pervaded by the imagery of illness, disability, and twisted bones. The last part, written after Melville had begun to recover, has more of the tone of Shakespearean comedy with its hero in motley, playing the role of Touchstone. Melville in fact had returned to Shakespeare and had found in him, as the introductory sketch for the collection of *Piazza Tales* (published before *The Confidence Man* was completed) indicates, a means of relief and escape from bitterness. But the dramatic intensity which Shakespeare had inspired in *Moby Dick* was gone.

Melville, at the age of thirty-seven, seemed worn out. He had sold the productive half of his farm in the spring of 1856, and his family was worried about his health. Judge Shaw agreed to finance a trip to Europe and the Holy Land, and Melville left on October 11 for Scotland, England (where he saw Hawthorne), and the Mediterranean; and he returned on May 20, 1857, with restored energy and the full notebook that his father-in-law doubtless hoped for. But he was not to return to writing. The firm of Dix and Edwards, which had been the most recent of his publishers, had been dissolved; and although he was invited to contribute to the new *Atlantic Monthly* he was persuaded that lecturing would be more profitable. Accordingly, for three years, he traveled the lecture circuit, going as far south as Tennessee and as far west as Chicago and Wisconsin, talking about "Roman Statuary," "The South Seas," and "Traveling — Its Pleasures and Pains." But he was not successful on the platform, and soon after the beginning of his third season he gave it up and decided to make a trip around the world on a sailing ship captained by his younger brother Tom.

He had amused himself by writing verses before he left, and he left behind a volume of poems for Elizabeth to publish if she could. Neither the volume nor the trip, however, materialized. The ship was indefinitely delayed in San Francisco, and Melville was home-

sick enough to hurry home by steamer. After the outbreak of the
Civil War he tried in vain for a commission in the Navy and
eventually managed to sell the rest of his Pittsfield property and
move to New York City where he continued to write verses about
the progress of the war. By the end of the hostilities he had almost
enough to make a volume, and he filled it out and published,
through the Harpers in 1866, *Battle-Pieces and Aspects of the War*
with a prose supplement advocating peaceful reconciliation with
the South. Although there was no question about his firm Union
sympathies, the poems and the supplement were sufficiently de-
tached from the strong political feelings of the day to make him
properly eligible, during a period of reform, for an appointment
to a position he had been seeking for some years — that of deputy
inspector in the New York Customhouse. He received it in the
early winter of 1866 and held it for nearly twenty years.

During these years Melville continued to be quietly but unpro-
fessionally interested in writing. Poetry seemed to be the best
means he found for occupying his mind, and the quantity of it increased as he filled the numerous quarter sheets he could con-
veniently carry around in his coat pocket. In 1870 he began buying
books again (a sure symptom, in him, of literary activity) and in
1875 his secret could no longer be kept: "pray do not mention to
any one that he is writing poetry," Elizabeth wrote her mother
after revealing it, " — you know how such things spread and he
would be very angry if he knew I had spoken of it." Yet within
the confidence of the family his uncle Peter Gansevoort heard the
report and generously offered to subsidize the publication of Melville's most ambitious work — a narrative poem of about eighteen
thousand lines called *Clarel: A Poem and Pilgrimage in the Holy
Land*.

Clarel was supposed to be a philosophical poem, based on Melville's own pilgrimage of nineteen years before, dealing with a

young man's search for religious faith. But its imaginative design
is that of a novel. The plot centers on a wandering pilgrimage
undertaken by Clarel and a group of companions while he is
waiting for his sweetheart Ruth to pass through a period of
mourning for the death of her father. The time is between the
symbolic dates of Epiphany and Ash Wednesday, and the climax
occurs when Clarel returns to Jerusalem and finds that Ruth, too,
has died and that such wisdom and faith as he has acquired must
be subject to the test of deep and bitter emotion. And within this
framework of design Melville placed the most extraordinary and
interesting group of characters he had ever created: the mysterious
hunchbacked Roman, Celio; Nathan, the Puritan Zionist from
Illinois; the American recluse, Vine, who resembled Hawthorne;
Nehemiah, the gentle, saintly version of Captain Ahab who had
learned to accept the universe; the misanthropic Swede, Mortmain;
Ungar, the embittered Confederate, with American Indian blood;
the smoothly armored Anglican priest, Derwent; the eager believer,
Rolfe, who was more bronzed in body than in mind and may have
been an ironic partial portrait of Melville himself; and a score or
more of others representing many nationalities and beliefs. Melville's interest in people and his knowledge of mankind had ob-
viously increased enormously since he had quit writing fiction.

More significantly, though, he had become less interested in absolute truth and the means of attaining it than he had been in his
youth. The conflict which had created the dramatic tension in
Moby Dick had, in the course of a quarter century, become for him
almost conventionally symbolized in the controversy between
religion and science; and, although he used this at length in his
poem, it no longer seriously bothered him. The psychological interests which had emerged in *Pierre* had become stronger and more
diverse. He was more interested in the kinds of people who could
believe such a variety of things with such great ranges of intensity.

Human beings would always find symbols for their emotions of faith and despair, he decided, and inspiration, observation, and introspection were simply different means of obtaining emotional satisfaction and not conflicting ways to "truth."

In the light of this change in the direction of Melville's imaginative development it seems a pity that he did not write his poetry early and his novels late in life. For *Clarel*, fascinating though it is in many respects, is not a great or even a good poem. The major characters are entirely too discursive, and their discourse is often hard to follow in the jingling octosyllabics in which most of it is composed. It was less designed for popularity, in fact, than any other of Melville's works; and when it appeared, in two volumes, on June 3, 1876, it was almost completely ignored.

Yet a return to print had a stimulating effect on Melville, and although he was almost a completely forgotten author he spent a good deal of time during the last years of his life gathering his literary resources. He had poems from his last years in the Berkshires, poems from his trip abroad that he called "Fruit of Travel Long Ago," and other poems called "Sea Pieces" that he had written from time to time. He was also experimenting and was to continue to experiment with prose sketches of picturesque individuals and appropriate poems to go with them. Near the end of his life he was to publish two small volumes of verse in limited editions of twenty-five copies for his friends (*John Marr and Other Sailors* in 1888, and *Timoleon* in 1891) and was to collect and organize for publication at least two more. The best of the poems are those that preserve or seem to preserve the fresh emotions of some special occasion or the retrospective pieces (such as "After the Pleasure Party," among the longer ones) of a man who continued to be puzzled by the many mysteries of life but had become content to make the best of his own. Yet his final burst of creative energy and one of the finest works of his imagination was not in the form of

41

poetry but in the prose fiction he had completely neglected for over a generation.

Billy Budd, Foretopman differs from Melville's earlier novels because it was a mature and successfully controlled outgrowth of the inquisitiveness about human behavior which made *Clarel* so remarkable. It developed out of one of his experiments in combining prose and verse, such as the one he published as "John Marr" — an introductory sketch of a remarkably handsome young sailor who was condemned to be hanged as the ringleader of an incipient mutiny and who expressed his last sentiments in a ballad composed on the eve of the execution. But Billy, as he crept into Melville's imagination with all the physical signs of noble birth, seems to have been difficult to sketch. He appears to have first been imagined as guilty and then as innocent of the charge, and the conception of innocence was the germ from which the story grew. Why should an innocent man be hanged? The best inference to be drawn from the surviving working manuscript is that Melville's first impulse was to answer that he was a victim of another man's wickedness. He had personally known, if the record of *White Jacket* can be trusted, a ship's master-at-arms with an evil sadistic genius beneath a bland exterior, and he was acutely aware of the power for evil that a malicious person in such a position might possess. Out of his memory and still-indignant awareness he created the character of John Claggert who was to accuse the innocent Billy of a crime and be killed by a spontaneous blow from the speechless sailor. And for this, under the Articles of War, Billy had to be hanged.

Yet Melville had learned that the world was far too complex to be pictured in black and white. Evil and goodness might exist side by side, as he made clear in the almost allegorical exaggeration of these qualities in Claggart and Billy, but reality was in between. Billy had not struck "through the mask" of anything (as Ahab had tried to do) by hitting Claggart. Justice was not absolute, as Pierre had believed, but man-made. Billy had to be hanged not as a matter of course but by decision of court-martial. And Melville also had within his experience a court-martial such as Billy would have had to endure: his cousin, Guert Gansevoort, had presided over such a one under the direction of Captain Alexander Mackenzie of the brig *Somers* in 1842 and had hanged the son of the secretary of war on a similar charge. The affair had created a scandal which was being revived at the time Melville was working on the *Billy Budd* manuscript and it was still a family mystery that Guert should have been almost broken by his action while insisting that it "was *approved* of God." Here was a mystery that appealed to the mature Melville more than the mystery of Iago.

So, as his manuscript went through its various later stages of painful revision, he created the character of Captain Vere, master of H.M.S. *Indomitable* (or *Bellipotent*, as he finally decided to call it) during the Napoleonic wars, who resembled both Guert Gansevoort and Captain Mackenzie and was a wise and good man who loved Billy as a son but forced a reluctant court to condemn him to death. He talked privately with Billy to such effect that Billy died with the words "God bless Captain Vere" on his lips. But the captain was not blessed. He was haunted. He himself died murmuring the words — though not in accents of remorse — "Billy Budd, Billy Budd."

Billy Budd has almost as many meanings to as many readers as *Moby Dick*, and perhaps for the same reasons. It has the hidden ambivalence of any work of art which grows by accretion rather than by design, the ambiguity that is found in any intelligent and honest attempt to solve a profound problem of human behavior, and the power which an author only manages to get into a book when he succeeds in capturing in his own person the major tensions of his age. For the problem that bothered Melville in *Billy*

Budd was not the problem of knowledge that had worried him in his youth. It was the problem of man. Is he a social being, responsible to the welfare of the society to which he belongs? Or is he an independent moral individual, responsible to his private awareness of guilt and innocence? This was the dilemma Captain Vere faced when, in Melville's fiction, the preservation of discipline in the British fleet was absolutely requisite to the preservation of England's freedom. Melville's solution was to make him behave as a social being but pay a penalty by suffering the private agonies of his private conscience.

The problem, however, was not a fictitious one. When Melville finished the last revision of his manuscript, on April 19, five months before his death in 1891, society had become far more complex than it had been when he dealt with the validity of individual awareness in *Moby Dick* forty years before. *Billy Budd* was not to be published until 1924, many years after its author's death. But the problem with which it dealt has not lessened with the passing years. Man's relationship to his private self and to the society in which he dwells is still the greatest source of tension of modern times. And Herman Melville's strongest claim to greatness is that his imaginative development kept abreast of the times — despite neglect and adversity and more than one failure, the acuteness and depth of his sensitivity never failed.

♪ Selected Bibliography

Collected Editions of Herman Melville's Work

The Works of Herman Melville, 12 volumes (London: Constable, 1922–23), with 4 supplementary volumes of poetry and posthumous prose (1924), is the most complete edition of Melville yet issued.

Complete Works (Chicago and New York: Hendricks House) is in two editions, a trade edition with editorial notes and a subscribers' edition with additional textual notes. It includes *Collected Poems*, edited by H. P. Vincent (1947); *Piazza Tales*, edited by E. S. Oliver (1948); *Pierre*, edited by H. A. Murray (1949); *Moby Dick*, edited by L. S. Mansfield and H. P. Vincent (1952); *The Confidence Man*, edited by Elizabeth Foster (1954); *Clarel*, edited by W. E. Bezanson (1960).

Original American Editions

Typee: A Peep at Polynesian Life. New York: Wiley and Putnam, 1846.
Omoo. New York: Harper, 1847.
Mardi and a Voyage Thither. New York: Harper, 1849.
Redburn: His First Voyage. New York: Harper, 1849.
White Jacket; or, The World in a Man-of-War. New York: Harper, 1850.
Moby Dick; or, The Whale. New York: Harper, 1851.
Pierre; or, The Ambiguities. New York: Harper, 1852.
Israel Potter, His Forty Years of Exile. New York: Putnam, 1855.
Piazza Tales. New York: Putnam, 1856.
The Confidence Man, His Masquerade. New York: Dix, Edwards, 1857.
Battle-Pieces and Aspects of the War. New York: Harper, 1866.
Clarel: A Poem and Pilgrimage in the Holy Land. New York: Putnam, 1876.
John Marr and Other Sailors. New York: De Vinne, 1888.
Timoleon. New York: Caxton, 1891.
The Apple Tree Table and Other Sketches. Princeton, N.J.: Princeton University Press, 1922.
Shorter Novels of Herman Melville. New York: Liveright, 1928. (Includes *Billy Budd*, first published in London by Constable in 1924.)

Journals and Correspondence

"Journal of Melville's Voyage in a Clipper Ship," *New England Quarterly*, 2:120–39 (January 1929).

Journal of a Visit to London and the Continent by Herman Melville, edited by Eleanor M. Metcalf. Cambridge, Mass.: Harvard University Press, 1948.

Melville's Journal of a Visit to Europe and the Levant, October 11, 1856–May 6, 1857, edited by Howard C. Horsford. Princeton, N.J.: Princeton University Press, 1955.

Family Correspondence of Herman Melville, 1830–1904, edited by V. H. Palsits. New York: New York Public Library, 1929.

The Letters of Herman Melville, edited by Merrell R. Davis and William H. Gilman. New Haven: Yale University Press, 1960.

Current American Reprints

Billy Budd and Piazza Tales. New York: Dolphin (Doubleday). $.95.

The Confidence Man. New York: Evergreen (Grove). $1.75.

Four Short Novels. New York: Bantam. $.50.

His Fifty Years of Exile (Israel Potter). New York: American Century (Sagamore). $1.25.

Moby Dick, New York: Books, Inc. $1.65. New York: Collins (Norton). $1.25. New York: Dolphin. $1.45. New York: Everyman (Dutton). $2.95. New York: Grosset and Dunlap. $1.98. New York: Harper. $1.60. New York: Laurel (Dell). $.75. New York: Modern Library (Random House). $.75 (paper); $1.95 (cloth); $2.95 (Giant, Rockwell Kent, illustrator). New York: Oxford. $2.50 (whaling illustrations). New York: Pocket Books. $.35. New York: Rinehart. $.95. * New York: Riverside (Houghton Mifflin). $.85. New York: Signet (New American Library). $.50.

Pierre. New York: Evergreen. $2.95.

* *The Portable Melville.* New York: Viking. $2.95.

* *Redburn.* New York: Anchor (Doubleday). $.95.

Selected Tales and Poems. New York: Rinehart. $.95.

Selected Writings. New York: Modern Library. $2.95.

Selections. New York: American Book. $2.00.

Shorter Novels. Greenwich, Conn.: Premier (Fawcett). $.50. * New York: Universal (Grosset and Dunlap). $1.25.

Typee. New York: Bantam. $.50. New York: Books, Inc. $1.65. New York: Everyman. $1.95 (second American edition). New York: Grosset and Dunlap. $1.98. New York: Harper. $1.40. New York: Oxford. $1.65.

Typee and Billy Budd. New York: Everyman. $1.75.

White Jacket. New York: Evergreen. $1.95.

* Editions preceded by an asterisk are available in paperback in England under the Mayflower imprint; Evergreen editions are also available in England.

Selected Bibliography

Biographical and Critical Studies

Anderson, C. R. *Melville in the South Seas*. New York: Columbia University Press, 1939.
Arvin, Newton. *Herman Melville*. New York: Sloane, 1950.
Bowen, Merlin. *The Long Encounter: Self and Experience in the Writings of Herman Melville*. Chicago: University of Chicago Press, 1960.
Chase, Richard. *Herman Melville*. New York: Macmillan, 1949.
Davis, M. R. *Melville's Mardi: A Chartless Voyage*. New Haven: Yale University Press, 1952.
Gilman, W. H. *Melville's Early Life and Redburn*. New York: New York University Press, 1951.
Howard, Leon. *Herman Melville: A Biography*. Berkeley and Los Angeles: University of California Press, 1951.
James, C. L. R. *Mariners, Renegades, and Castaways*. New York: James, 1953.
Leyda, Jay. *The Melville Log: A Documentary Life of Herman Melville, 1819–1891*. 2 volumes. New York: Harcourt, Brace, 1951.
Mason, Ronald. *The Spirit above the Dust: A Study of Herman Melville*. London: John Lehmann, 1951.
Metcalf, Eleanor M. *Herman Melville: Cycle and Epicycle*. Cambridge, Mass.: Harvard University Press, 1953.
Mumford, Lewis. *Herman Melville*. New York: Harcourt, Brace, 1929.
Olson, Charles. *Call Me Ishmael*. New York: Reynal and Hitchcock, 1947.
Sedgwick, W. E. *Herman Melville: The Tragedy of Mind*. Cambridge, Mass.: Harvard University Press, 1944.
Simon, Jean. *Herman Melville, marin, métaphysicien et poète*. Paris: Boivin, 1939.
Stern, M. R. *The Fine Hammered Steel of Herman Melville*. Urbana: University of Illinois Press, 1957.
Stone, Geoffrey. *Melville*. New York: Sheed and Ward, 1949.
Thorp, Willard. *Herman Melville*. New York: American Book, 1938.
Weaver, R. M. *Herman Melville, Mariner and Mystic*. New York: Doran, 1921.

Special Topics

Braswell, William. *Melville's Religious Thought*. Durham: Duke University Press, 1943.
Hetherington, H. W. *Melville's Reviewers, British and American, 1846–1891*. Chapel Hill: University of North Carolina Press, 1961.
Hillway, Tyrus, ed. *Moby Dick Centennial Essays*. Dallas, Texas: Southern Methodist University Press, 1953.
Lanzinger, Klaus. *Primitivismus und Naturalismus im Prosaschaffen Herman Melvilles*. Innsbruck: Universitätsverlag Wagner, 1959.

Percival, M. O. *A Reading of Moby Dick*. Chicago: University of Chicago Press, 1950.

Pommer, H. E. *Milton and Melville*. Pittsburgh: University of Pittsburgh Press, 1955.

Rosenberry, E. H. *Melville and the Comic Spirit*. Cambridge, Mass.: Harvard University Press, 1955.

Sealts, M. M., Jr. *Melville's Reading: A Check-List of Books Owned and Borrowed*. Cambridge, Mass.: Offprinted from *Harvard Library Bulletin*, 1948–1950.

―――. *Melville as Lecturer*. Cambridge, Mass.: Harvard University Press, 1957.

Stafford, W. T., ed. *Melville's Billy Budd and the Critics*. San Francisco: Wadsworth, 1961.

Stern, M. R., ed. *Discussions of Moby Dick*. Boston: Heath, 1960.

Sundermann, K. H. *Herman Melvilles Gedankengut*. Berlin, 1937.

Thompson, Lawrance. *Melville's Quarrel with God*. Princeton, N.J.: Princeton University Press, 1952.

Vincent, H. P. *The Trying Out of Moby Dick*. Boston: Houghton Mifflin, 1949.

Wright, Nathalia. *Melville's Use of the Bible*. Durham: Duke University Press, 1949.

NOTE: This essay is especially indebted to two important but unpublished studies of Melville: the scholarly edition of the working manuscript and finished text of *Billy Budd* by Harrison Hayford and Merton Sealts, Jr., and Hayford's study of Melville's imagery.

70
71
72
74
75
76
77
79
83
85
89